Contents

This Report reviews developments in international economic and exchange rate policies and is submitted pursuant to the Omnibus Trade and Competitiveness Act of 1988, 22 U.S.C. § 5305, and Section 701 of the Trade Facilitation and Trade Enforcement Act of 2015, 19 U.S.C. § 4421.[1]

---

[1] The Treasury Department has consulted with the Board of Governors of the Federal Reserve System and International Monetary Fund management and staff in preparing this Report.

Executive Summary

This Report is the first to implement the intensified evaluation provisions of the Trade Facilitation and Trade Enforcement Act of 2015 (the "Act"). The provisions of the Act provide the United States with valuable new reporting and monitoring tools, as well as new measures to address unfair currency practices. The Act establishes a process to monitor key indicators related to foreign exchange operations, engage economies that may be pursuing unfair practices, and impose meaningful penalties on economies that fail to adopt appropriate policies. The legislation accomplishes these important goals in a way that is consistent with our international obligations.

The new reporting and monitoring tools designed under the Act significantly enhance Treasury's ability to undertake a data-driven, objective analysis of an economy's foreign exchange policies and their impact on bilateral trade with the United States and the broader multilateral trade position. The Act sets up a process in which Treasury delineates clear, objective criteria -- based on relevant economic indicators -- to determine whether an economy may be pursuing foreign exchange policies that could give it an unfair competitive advantage against the United States.

The Act requires that Treasury undertake an enhanced analysis of exchange rates and externally-oriented policies for each major trading partner that has: (1) a significant bilateral trade surplus with the United States, (2) a material current account surplus, and (3) engaged in persistent one-sided intervention in the foreign exchange market. Drawing on economic research and our own analysis of the data, Treasury has determined the thresholds for these criteria as follows (see Section 3 for details):

1) An economy has a significant trade surplus with the United States if its bilateral trade surplus is larger than $20 billion (roughly 0.1 percent of U.S. GDP) which captures around 80 percent of the value of all trade surpluses with the United States last year.

2) An economy has a material current account surplus if its surplus is larger than 3.0 percent of that economy's GDP.

3)   An economy has engaged in persistent one-sided intervention in the foreign exchange market if it has conducted *repeated* net purchases of foreign currency that amount to more than 2 percent of its GDP over the year.

In determining the appropriate factors to assess these criteria, Treasury took a thorough approach, analyzing data spanning 15 years across dozens of economies, including all economies that have had a trade surplus with the United States during that period, and which in the aggregate represent about 80 percent of global GDP. <u>The thresholds are relatively robust in that reasonable changes to the thresholds do not materially change the Report's conclusions. Treasury will also continue to review the factors it uses to assess these criteria to ensure that the new reporting and monitoring tools provided under the Act meet the objective of indicating where unfair currency practices may be emerging.</u>

Pursuant to the Act, Treasury finds that no economy currently satisfies all three criteria, however, five major trading partners of the United States met two of the three criteria for enhanced analysis. <u>Treasury is creating a new "Monitoring List" that includes these economies: China, Japan, Korea, Taiwan, and Germany</u>. China, Japan, Germany, and Korea are identified as a result of a material current account surplus combined with a significant bilateral trade surplus with the United States. Taiwan is identified as a result of its material current account surplus and its persistent, one-sided intervention in foreign exchange markets. Treasury will closely monitor and assess the economic trends and foreign exchange policies of these economies.

The provisions in this bipartisan legislation are an important complement to the Administration's ongoing efforts to better protect American workers and firms. If an economy meets all three criteria, the President, through the Secretary of the Treasury, is required to commence enhanced bilateral engagement with that country. If, one year after the start of enhanced bilateral engagement, the Secretary determines that the country has failed to adopt appropriate policies to correct its undervaluation and external surpluses, the President is required to take one or more of the following actions: (1) denying access to OPIC financing; (2) excluding the country from U.S. government procurement; (3) calling for heightened IMF surveillance; and (4) instructing the United States Trade Representative to take into account such failure to adopt appropriate policies in assessing whether to enter into a trade agreement or initiate or participate in trade agreement negotiations. The President may waive the remedial action requirement under specified circumstances.

The State of the Global Economy

<u>Underpinned by robust job creation and resilient domestic demand, the U.S. economy grew at a solid pace of 2.4 percent in 2015. Outside of the United States, growth in other advanced economies was more disappointing and emerging market economies are facing significant headwinds from low commodity prices, weak trade growth, and internal cyclical dynamics. Most projections for 2016 point to the continuation of modest growth.</u> Growth in Europe also has picked up, albeit from a very low level, but demand in many parts of Europe remains tepid. Demand also remains weak in Japan, with consumption especially hit hard following the April 2014 hike in the consumption tax.

Demand has also been weaker than usual in many emerging market economies, most notably in China, where a necessary but difficult transition is taking place from investment and export-led growth to consumer-led growth. Concern that growth is decelerating in emerging markets has resulted in large capital outflows from these economies and downward pressure on their currencies. The relative strength of the U.S. economy has pushed the dollar stronger against many currencies and on a trade-weighted basis over the past year and a half. The related softness in foreign demand has exerted a drag on U.S. growth. Many emerging market central banks have intervened in currency markets over the past year to prevent their currencies from depreciating even further against the U.S. dollar, and this has led to a sharp reduction in global foreign exchange reserves. Financial markets were unusually volatile in the context of the change in China's exchange rate policy last August, and uncertain growth prospects in China, with falling oil prices amplifying some of the market volatility.

The lower price of oil has had a large impact on the redistribution of current account balances globally. Oil importing economies have benefitted, and in some cases—China, Germany, Taiwan, and Korea—have seen their already large external surpluses become even larger, while some oil exporting countries have encountered serious financial challenges.

More support is needed globally to bolster global demand and help stabilize growth expectations. The Administration has strongly advocated, bilaterally and multilaterally, that economies should use all available policy tools to boost demand. In February 2016 and again in April, the G-20 Finance Ministers and Central Bank Governors endorsed this view, stating that G-20 countries "will use all policy tools—monetary, fiscal and structural—individually and collectively" to foster confidence and preserve and strengthen the recovery.

Global growth is being held back by (1) still-high private sector leverage in some economies, (2) inadequate macroeconomic support, and (3) sluggish lending growth in some economies. Weak investment is often cited as a contributing factor to subdued global growth, but investment tends to follow, rather than lead GDP growth in the first instance. Still, policies to lift private investment as well as public investment could help spur global demand. Trade growth also has decelerated. More policy action is needed globally to strengthen demand. Monetary policy responses have been forceful in general, but they need to be supported with additional fiscal actions to deliver a stronger boost to domestic demand. Exceptionally low long-term interest rates provide governments with more fiscal breathing room than under historically normal circumstances. Increased infrastructure investment could be especially powerful, as it would boost near-term demand while also strengthening potential growth in the longer-term. And there are a number of advanced and emerging market economies with large external surpluses, including Germany, China, Korea, and Taiwan, that could bolster domestic demand and contribute both to stronger global growth and a more balanced global economy.

Treasury Assessments of Major Trading Partners

As noted above, Treasury is creating a new "Monitoring List" that cites major trading partners that have met two of the three criteria specified in the Act. In this first Report, the Monitoring List includes China, Japan, Korea, Taiwan, and Germany. Regarding these economies:

- China has both a significant bilateral trade surplus with the United States and a material current account surplus. China has intervened heavily in the foreign exchange markets in recent months to *support* the RMB, after strong downward market pressure triggered by a surprise change in China's foreign exchange policy last August. Such a depreciation would have had negative consequences for the Chinese and global economies. More clarity over exchange rate goals, and that devaluation will not be used to support growth, would help stabilize the market. Treasury estimates that from August 2015 through March 2016, China sold more than $480 billion in foreign currency assets to support the value of the RMB. At the same time, China has a very large and growing bilateral goods trade surplus with the United States. This underscores the need for further implementation of structural reforms to rebalance the Chinese economy to household consumption, and for consumption-friendly fiscal stimulus to support demand.

- Japan has a significant bilateral trade surplus with the United States and a material current account surplus. Japan has not intervened in the foreign exchange market in over four years. Given Japan's fragile growth outlook, it is increasingly important that the authorities use all policy levers, including a flexible fiscal policy and an ambitious structural reform agenda, to lift near-term growth. Treasury assesses that current conditions in the dollar-yen foreign exchange market are orderly, and reiterates the importance of all countries adhering to their G-20 and G-7 commitments regarding exchange rate policies.

- Korea has a significant bilateral trade surplus with the United States and a material current account surplus. Treasury estimates that during the second half of 2015 through March 2016, the Korean authorities intervened to resist depreciation of the won during periods of financial market turbulence, selling an estimated $26 billion in foreign exchange, including activity in the forward and swaps market. This represented a shift from several years of asymmetric intervention to resist appreciation. Appreciation of the won over the medium-term would help Korea reorient its economy away from its current reliance on exports by encouraging the reallocation of resources to the non-tradables sector. Treasury has urged Korea to limit its foreign exchange intervention only to circumstances of disorderly market conditions. In addition, we encourage the Korean authorities to increase the transparency of their foreign exchange operations and take further steps to support domestic demand.

- Taiwan has a material current account surplus and, per Treasury estimates, has engaged in persistent net foreign currency purchases through most of 2015. In light of Taiwan's large current account surplus, such interventions are concerning. Taiwan's bilateral trade surplus with the United States, however, was not significant at less than $15 billion in 2015, and thus Taiwan did not meet all three criteria the Act establishes to advance to enhanced analysis and engagement. Nonetheless, the authorities should limit foreign exchange interventions to the exceptional circumstances of disorderly market conditions, as well as increase the transparency of reserve holdings and foreign exchange market intervention.

- Germany has both a significant bilateral trade surplus with the United States and a material current account surplus. Germany's 2015 current account surplus, at almost $290 billion, accounted for the bulk of the euro area's surplus, and pushed the surplus of the euro zone to over 3 percent of GDP. The European Central Bank (ECB) has not intervened in foreign currency markets since 2011, and did so then as part of a G-7 concerted intervention to stabilize the yen following Japan's earthquake and tsunami[2]. Nonetheless, Germany has the second largest current account surplus globally. This represents substantial excess saving—more than 8 percent of GDP—that could, at least in part, be used to support German domestic demand, while reducing the current account surplus and contributing markedly to euro-area and global rebalancing. In Treasury's view, Germany has adequate policy space to provide additional support to demand.

While no economy met all three of the criteria, this result is a reflection, in part, of the dynamics of the global economy during the past year, in which capital outflows from emerging markets have led a number of economies to engage in foreign exchange intervention to resist further *depreciation* of their currency (rather than appreciation). The extent of these flows was unusually high by historical standards, which underscores the possibility that more economies may trigger these thresholds going forward.

Based on the analysis in this Report, Treasury has also concluded that no major trading partner of the United States met the standard of manipulating the rate of exchange between its currency and the United States dollar for purposes of preventing effective balance of payments adjustments or gaining unfair

---

[2] For the purposes of Section 701 of the Act, policies of the ECB, which holds responsibility for monetary policy for the euro area, will be assessed as the monetary authority of individual euro area countries.

competitive advantage in international trade during the period covered in the Report.[3]

The Administration shares strongly the objective of taking aggressive and effective actions to ensure a level playing field for our workers and companies. The President has been clear that no economy should grow its exports based on a persistently undervalued exchange rate, and Treasury has been working aggressively to address exchange rate issues bilaterally, including through the U.S.-China Strategic and Economic Dialogue, and multilaterally through the G-7, G-20, and the International Monetary Fund.

This strategy has produced results. The United States has secured commitments from the G-20 member countries to move more rapidly to more market-determined exchange rates, avoid persistent exchange rate misalignments, refrain from competitive exchange rate devaluations, and not target exchange rates for competitive purposes. Through Treasury's leadership, the G-7 member countries, including Japan, have publicly affirmed that their fiscal and monetary policies will be oriented toward domestic objectives using domestic instruments. Treasury has also pushed for stronger IMF surveillance of the exchange rate policy obligations of its members. The IMF now publishes an exchange rate assessment for 29 economies, and is improving its exchange rate analysis in its Article IV reports on member countries. And through U.S. leadership, the Trans-Pacific Partnership countries have adopted—for the first time in the context of a trade agreement—provisions that address unfair currency practices by explicitly adopting G-20 exchange rate commitments and by promoting transparency and accountability.

Treasury will continue to closely monitor adherence to all G-7, G-20, and IMF exchange rate commitments. These include the G-7 commitments to orient fiscal and monetary policies towards domestic objectives using domestic instruments and to not target exchange rates, and the G-20 commitments to avoid persistent exchange rate misalignments and to not target exchange rates for competitive purposes. It also includes G-7 and G-20 commitments to consult closely on exchange market issues.

---

[3] As defined by Section 3004 of the Omnibus Trade and Competitiveness Act of 1988.

Treasury will also continue to review the factors it uses to assess whether an economy has (1) a significant bilateral trade surplus with the United States, (2) a material current account surplus, and (3) engaged in persistent one-sided intervention in the foreign exchange market, to ensure these new reporting and monitoring tools meet their objective of indicating where unfair currency practices may be emerging.

Section 1: Global Economic and External Developments

Context

The Omnibus Trade and Competitiveness Act of 1988 and the Trade Facilitation and Trade Enforcement Act of 2015 (the "Act") require the Secretary of the Treasury to provide semiannual reports to Congress on the international economic and exchange rate policies of the major trading partners of the United States. Taken together, these acts require that the Report consider whether any major trading partner has met all of the three following criteria: (1) a significant bilateral trade surplus with the United States; (2) a material current account surplus; and (3) persistent one-sided intervention in the foreign exchange market, as indicated by the assessment factors described in Section 3 of this Report, and "whether countries manipulate the rate of exchange between their currency and the United States dollar for purposes of preventing effective balance of payments adjustments or gaining unfair competitive advantage in international trade."

This Report assesses our major trading partners on the criteria used to determine whether an economy should receive enhanced analysis under the Act.[4] This Report also reviews the macroeconomic and exchange rate policies of a dozen of the largest trading partners of the United States,[5] accounting for around 70 percent of U.S. foreign trade, and assesses global economic developments more broadly. This Report covers developments in the second half of 2015, and where pertinent and available, data through end-March 2016, in order to assess whether economies manipulate the rate of exchange between their currency

---

[4] The assessment is based on data covering the 12 months of 2015.
[5] Excluding major oil exporters.

and the U.S. dollar for purposes of preventing effective balance of payments adjustments or gaining unfair competitive advantage in international trade.

U.S. Domestic Economic Trends

In the first quarter of 2016 consumer spending growth slowed, and business fixed investment, inventory investment and net exports all subtracted from growth. Residential construction, however, was very strong and government spending added to overall growth. Economic growth can be variable from quarter to quarter, with each year showing both stronger quarters and weaker quarters. Notwithstanding the tepid pace of growth in the first quarter, the underlying strength of the U.S. economy remains intact. Job growth has remained strong, and the unemployment rate is close to its lowest level in more than seven years.

The Near-Term Outlook for the U.S. Economy Is Favorable

Although developments abroad are acting as a headwind and the level of inventories looks to be excessive, the U.S. economy is in a strong position to meet these challenges. Private forecasts point to a rebound in GDP growth in Q2 to more than 2 percent and expect that stronger pace to continue for the second half of the year, led by healthy growth of consumer spending, further recovery in the housing sector, and a small boost from government spending.

Fiscal Headwinds Have Diminished

The rapid pace of fiscal consolidation in recent years has weighed on economic activity in the United States, but it has moderated recently and, in the second half of 2015, federal government spending contributed 0.1 percentage point to GDP growth. State and local outlays contributed a similar amount to growth in the second half of 2015. For the entire year, federal outlays were essentially neutral for growth while state and local spending provided a small boost to the economy. Looking ahead, federal government spending is expected to make a positive contribution to GDP in 2016, and continued improvement in state and local government finances has laid the groundwork for that sector to be a small net positive for growth once again this year.

The Near-Term Outlook for the U.S. Economy Is Favorable

Although developments abroad are acting as a headwind, the U.S. economy is in a strong position to meet external challenges. The current outlook suggests that real GDP will expand at a solid pace through the end of 2016, led by healthy growth of consumer spending, further recovery in the housing sector, and a small boost from government spending. A consensus of private forecasters predicts that after a weak first quarter, growth will pick up to 2.3 percent in the second quarter and 2.4 percent in the second half of the year.

Labor Market Conditions Continued to Improve and Inflation Slowed

The pace of job creation remained strong during the second half of 2015, and the unemployment rate moved lower. Nonfarm payroll employment increased by 228,000 per month on average during the nine months ending in March 2016, compared with average monthly gains of 220,000 over the first six months of 2015. The unemployment rate has declined by 0.3 percentage point since June 2015, and in March 2016 stood at 5.0 percent. Other indicators of labor utilization, including the rate of involuntary part-time employment, have also improved since mid-2015 but are still elevated compared with pre-recession levels and suggest some slack remains in labor markets.

Inflation picked up in late 2015, but was still relatively low in early 2016. The consumer price index rose 0.9 percent during the year ending in March 2016, compared with a 0.1 decline during the year ending in March 2015. Core consumer inflation (excluding energy and food prices) was 2.2 percent over the year ending in March 2016, up from 1.8 percent during the same period a year earlier. Wage pressures remained subdued, although there is some evidence that compensation growth started to strengthen in late 2015. Average hourly earnings rose 2.3 percent over the twelve months ending in March 2016, stepping up slightly from gains averaging 2 percent from 2011 through 2014. However, the Employment Cost Index (ECI) for private-industry workers showed compensation rising 1.9 percent and wages rising 2.1 percent over the twelve months of 2015, roughly in line with gains of recent years.

Putting Public Finances on a Sustainable Path Remains a Priority

The federal budget deficit continued to narrow in FY 2015, declining to 2.5 percent of GDP from 2.8 percent of GDP in FY 2014. Since peaking in 2009, the deficit has fallen by 7.3 percentage points—the most rapid pace of fiscal consolidation for any six-year period since the demobilization following World War II. The Administration's FY 2017 Budget shows the deficit declining slightly further, to 2.3 percent of GDP, in FY 2018 and stabilizing at 2.6 percent of GDP from FY 2019 to FY 2026—well below the 40-year average of 3.2 percent of GDP. The primary deficit (non-interest outlays less receipts) will be eliminated by FY 2021, and will be roughly neutral thereafter and not add to the federal debt. Publicly-held debt as a share of the economy declined to 73.8 percent of GDP in FY 2015; it is projected to stabilize at 76.5 percent of GDP in FYs 2016 and 2017 and then decline gradually to 75.3 percent in FY 2026.

U.S. External Trends

Developments in the U.S. Current Account and Trade Balances

The U.S. current account deficit rose to 2.7 percent of GDP in 2015, up from 2.2 percent of GDP in 2014, but still well below the peak deficit of 5.8 percent of GDP in 2006. The deficit of goods trade widened by $17.8 billion in 2015 compared to 2014, as a sharp fall in the petroleum deficit—due to lower oil prices—was more than offset by a widening in the non-petroleum goods deficit. The surplus in services in 2015 fell as well, by $13.6 billion relative to 2014, as services imports growth edged out services exports growth. The largest driver of the widening current account deficit in 2015 came from a drop in the primary income (net factor income) surplus, which declined by nearly $47 billion as earnings declined on U.S. assets held abroad.

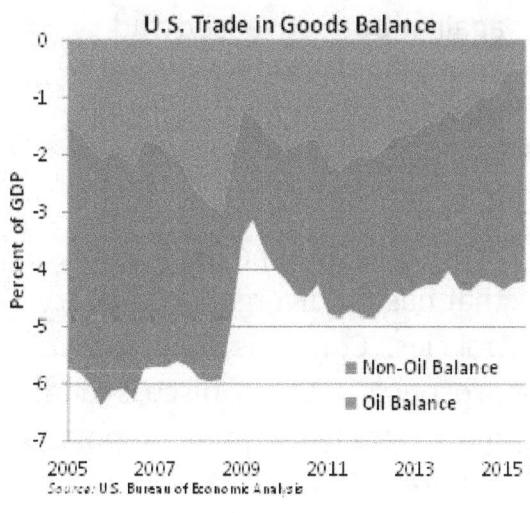

During 2015, two offsetting factors, low oil prices and weak conditions abroad, influenced the U.S. goods deficit. First, low oil prices helped shrink the U.S. petroleum deficit to $85 billion in 2015, a decrease of $104.7 billion relative to

2014. The oil deficit in terms of GDP was at its lowest level since 1998, at just 0.5 percent of GDP. This boost to the trade balance from oil was more than offset, however, by weak growth abroad and an associated stronger dollar, both of which contributed to a decrease in U.S. non-petroleum exports. Meanwhile, non-petroleum imports rose during this same period, driving the aggregate non-petroleum deficit higher by $122.6 billion, to roughly 3.8 percent of GDP. Overall, U.S. exports by volume decreased in 2015 by 0.5 percent compared a 2.5 percent increase in global trade.

At the end of the fourth quarter of 2015, the U.S. net international investment position stood at a deficit of $7.4 trillion (41 percent of GDP), a slight increase over the end-2014 position. The value of U.S.-owned foreign assets was $23.2 trillion, while value of foreign-owned U.S. assets stood at $30.6 trillion. Much of the recent deterioration over the past year has been driven by valuation effects that lowered the dollar value of U.S. assets held abroad.

The Dollar in Foreign Exchange Markets

The dollar continued to appreciate against both advanced and emerging market currencies in the second half of 2015, reflecting comparatively strong U.S. economic performance and prospects, and the implications that has for divergent monetary policies. Concerns about growth prospects in China, discussed in more detail later in the Report, generated considerable volatility in financial markets and caused several other currencies to

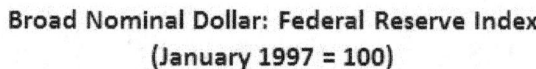

Broad Nominal Dollar: Federal Reserve Index (January 1997 = 100)

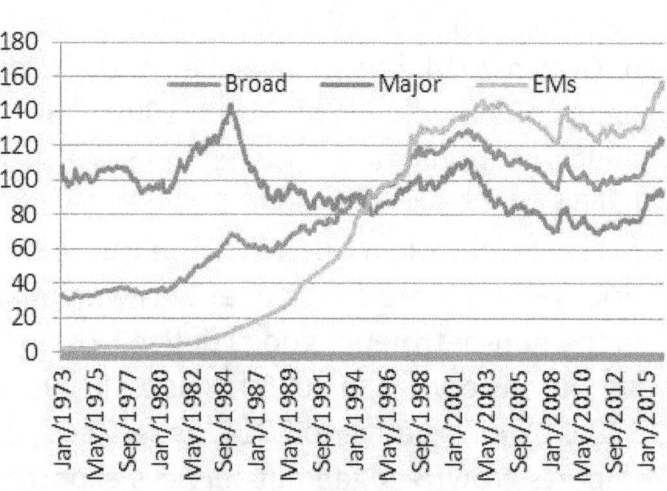

depreciate against the U.S. dollar. On a nominal, trade-weighted basis, the dollar appreciated 6.5 percent between end-June 2015 and end-December 2015. The dollar appreciated the most against the Brazilian *real*—by 27.3 percent between end-June 2015 and December 2015. Amid political uncertainty, Brazil has been hit hard by falling commodity prices that have exacerbated fiscal deficits, which in turn have complicated efforts to restrain high inflation. Declining oil prices have also put downward pressure on the Mexican peso, and falling commodity prices in general contributed to depreciation of the Canadian dollar against the U.S. dollar. The dollar rose 6.7 percent against the British pound amid weaker-than-expected economic data for the UK, shifting Bank of England policy expectations, and uncertainty over the future of the UK's membership in the European Union. Against the euro, the dollar's increase was more modest, 2.7 percent. Against the Japanese yen, the dollar *depreciated* by 1.5 percent.

Beginning in January 2016, the dollar began to depreciate against advanced economy currencies. During the first quarter of 2016, the dollar depreciated 2.9 percent on a nominal effective basis, reflecting a 4.9 percent decline against advanced economy currencies, particularly those of Japan and Canada. The dollar was flat against major emerging market trading partners as a group, but depreciated against the Brazilian *real* quite significantly.

International Economic Trends

The outlook for the global economy remains of concern, not least because the growth of aggregate demand has been modest and various high frequency indicators point to weaknesses. Starting with concerns over the pace of growth in China, and then turning to concerns over falling oil prices, renewed low inflation, deteriorating bank profits, and potentially worsening bank exposures, volatility in equity, bond, and currency markets rose substantially over the latter part of 2015 and into early 2016.

Global growth has decelerated, falling in 2015 to 3.1 percent, its lowest level in six years. The deceleration was driven by slower growth in emerging market economies. IMF data show that every developing economy region except Emerging and Developing Europe decelerated in 2015.[6] Advanced economies have fared only slightly better. As noted previously, growth in the United States is expected to accelerate. Growth in Europe also has

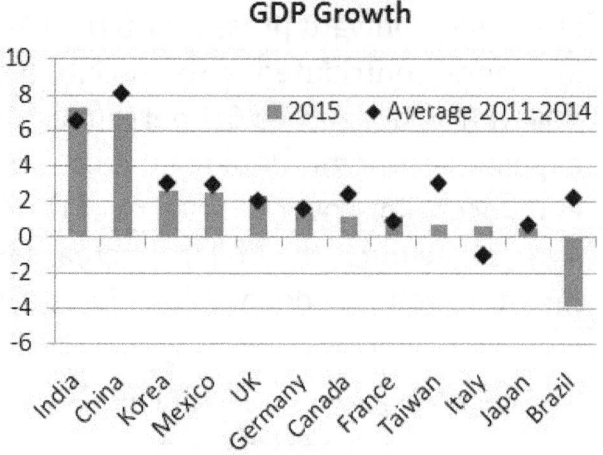

increased, though given how delayed and uneven it is, there remains scope in Europe for stronger growth with a stronger set of policy support. Growth in Japan has been highly variable and private consumption has been especially weak since the consumption tax was increased in April 2014.

Global current account imbalances have declined from their peak in 2007, but much of the decline reflects a contraction in demand on the part of some current account deficit economies rather than strong domestic demand growth in current account surplus economies. Several very large and persistent surpluses have widened further (Germany, Korea, Taiwan). In the absence of stronger domestic demand in the larger surplus economies, global growth has suffered and will continue to suffer if global adjustment

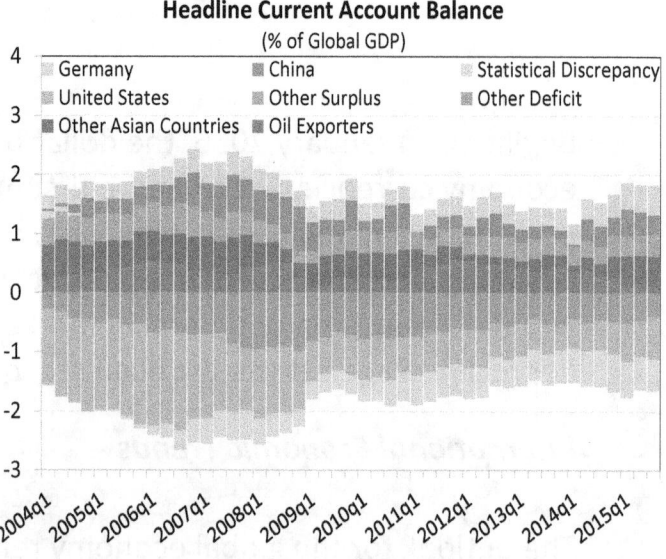

continues to occur mainly through weakened demand in the deficit economies.

---

[6] IMF World Economic Outlook Update, April 2016.

The large current account surpluses of Germany, China, Japan, Taiwan, and Korea all expanded in 2015, both in dollar terms and as shares of their GDP. Low oil prices played a significant role in these expanding surpluses, likely accounting for 2 percentage points of GDP or more of the growth in surpluses in these economies.

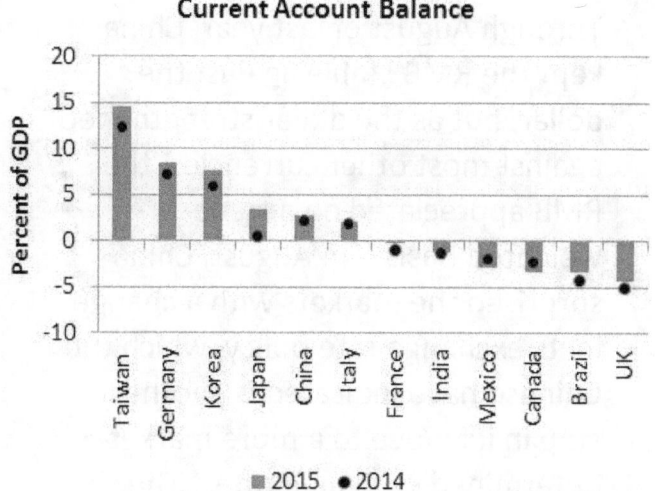

Current Account Balance

China

China's current account surplus for the second half of 2015 was $157 billion (2.8 percent of GDP), compared with $174 billion (3.1 percent of GDP) in the second half of 2014. Overall, the current account surplus grew to 3.1 percent of GDP ($331 billion) in 2015, up from 2.7 percent ($277 billion) in 2014, but well below its peak of 10 percent of GDP in 2007. The growing surplus was driven by lower nominal merchandise imports, reflecting a

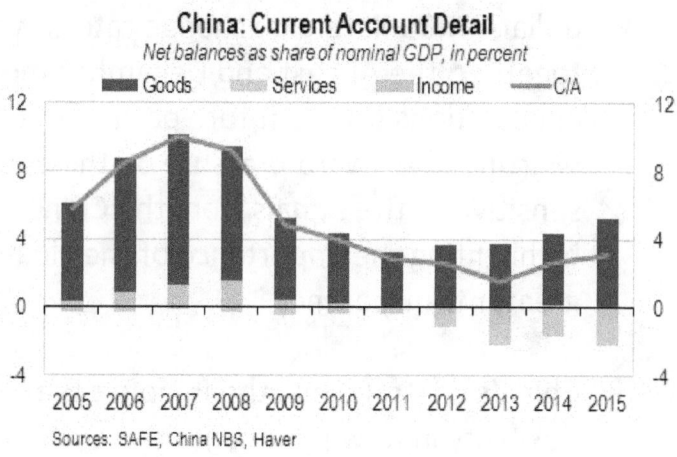

China: Current Account Detail
Net balances as share of nominal GDP, in percent

Sources: SAFE, China NBS, Haver

contraction in import volumes and falling commodity prices. Merchandise export volumes and values declined by 2.9 percent and 5.5 percent, respectively, in the second half of the year versus the second half of 2014. China's services deficit remained large, possibly reflecting disguised capital outflows. China runs a merchandise trade surplus and a services deficit with the United States. China's bilateral merchandise trade surplus was $365 billion in 2015, up from $343 billion in 2014, according to U.S. Census data. But the United States has a surplus of roughly $30 billion in its trade in services with China and, therefore, China's bilateral trade in goods and services balance with the United States is a bit lower.

Through August of last year, China kept the RMB stable against the dollar, but as the dollar strengthened against most other currencies, the RMB appreciated on a trade-weighted basis.[7] In August, China surprised the markets with a change in its exchange rate policy, which the Chinese have indicated is another step in its move to a more market-determined exchange rate. The policy shift resulted in RMB

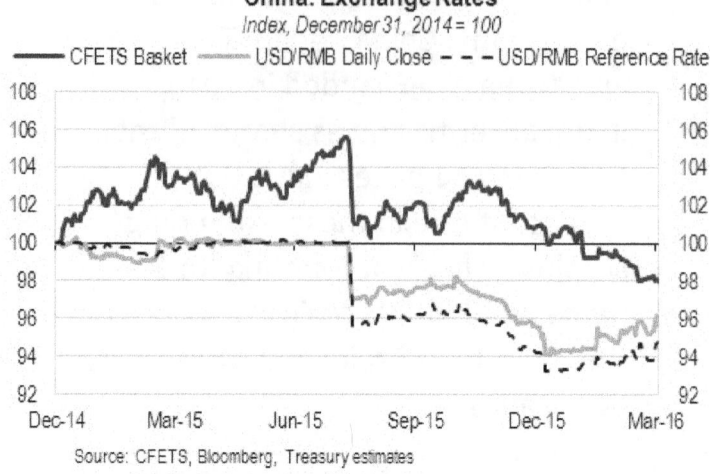

China: Exchange Rates
Index, December 31, 2014 = 100

— CFETS Basket ⋯⋯ USD/RMB Daily Close – – – USD/RMB Reference Rate

Source: CFETS, Bloomberg, Treasury estimates

depreciation of 3 percent against the dollar over two days. In December, the Chinese authorities sought to re-orient investor attention away from the U.S. dollar-RMB bilateral exchange rate toward a new trade-weighted measure. Taken together, the August and December measures effectively shifted market expectations for the future path of the RMB, and market forces are presently exerting downward pressure on the currency. Market participants remain highly sensitive to the signals from the Chinese authorities on the exchange rate, highlighting the importance of the clear communication of policy actions and greater transparency.

China's central bank, the People's Bank of China (PBOC), has sought to maintain flexibility in how it manages the exchange rate. It has also indicated that there is no basis for persistent RMB depreciation based on economic fundamentals. Stabilizing growth, including with fiscal policies that support consumption and lower China's high national savings rate, should be part of a policy mix that supports economic rebalancing and re-anchors expectations. Core factors that have been supportive of the RMB remain in place, including high net savings, strong external balances which include a sizeable and growing current account surplus, and improved terms of trade reflecting lower commodity prices. China has the tools to create the conditions for an orderly transition to a market-determined exchange rate. <u>Overall, the RMB should continue to experience real appreciation over the medium-term. Chinese authorities have stressed that the RMB will continue to be a strong currency, given China's current accounts surplus,</u>

---

[7] Equivalent to 6 percent nominal appreciation against a trade-weighted basket that the Chinese central bank introduced in December and published by the China Foreign Exchange Trade System (CFETS).

<u>higher economic growth, large foreign exchange reserves, and stable fiscal and financial conditions.</u>

Japan

Japan's current account surplus for the second half of 2015 reached $72.4 billion (3.5 percent of GDP), compared with $36.5 billion (1.7 percent of GDP) in the second half of 2014. For all of 2015, the current account surplus registered 3.3 percent of GDP, a substantial increase from 0.8 percent in 2014, driven by improvements in the trade balance due to lower oil prices and continued strong net foreign income (due in part to valuation effects stemming from the weaker yen).

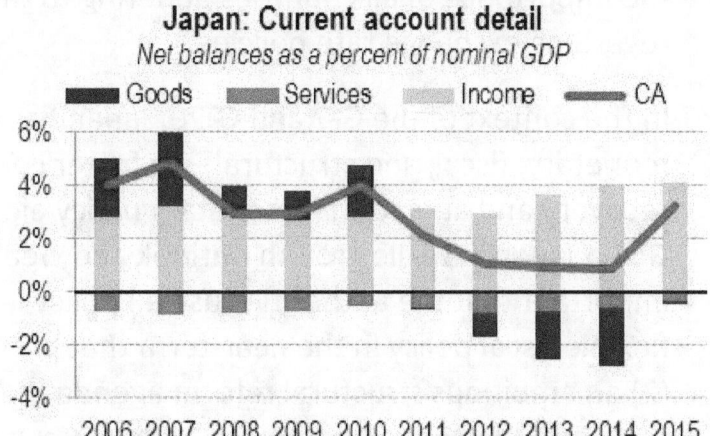

Japan: Current account detail
Net balances as a percent of nominal GDP

Source: Bank of Japan, Japan Ministry of Finance, Japan Cabinet Office. Figures are seasonally-adjusted and "Income" is primary income only.

In November, Japan recorded its first seasonally-adjusted trade surplus (goods and services) since March, but export volumes fell by 3.4 percent in the second half of 2015 as compared with the second half of 2014. Export volumes have continued to fall since reaching a peak at the end of 2014, dipping 0.8 percent in 2015 in part due to a contraction in shipments to China. At the same time, import volumes remain below their March 2014 peak, and declined in the last quarter of 2015.   Japan's merchandise trade surplus with the United States totaled $33.9 billion for the last six months through December, the third largest after China and Germany and on par with the same period one year earlier. Including services, Japan's overall trade surplus (merchandise *plus* services, seasonally adjusted) with the United States falls to $28.1 billion for the same period.

In January the Bank of Japan (BOJ) surprised markets by introducing negative interest rates on a portion of excess reserves, with BOJ Governor Kuroda saying the BOJ will continue to do whatever it takes to achieve its 2 percent inflation target. After initially depreciating in the days following the BOJ decision, the yen resumed its appreciation against the dollar and, as of end-March, stood 8.9 percent stronger since its recent low in mid-November. Japanese authorities characterized exchange rate movements as "quite rough" and said that they would "continue to watch the foreign exchange market with a sense of tension, and . . . act appropriately if that becomes necessary." Japan has not intervened in the foreign exchange market in over four years. Treasury assesses that current conditions in the dollar-yen foreign exchange market are orderly, and reiterates the importance of all countries adhering to their G-20 and G-7 commitments regarding exchange rate policies.[8]

In the context of the G-7 and G-20, Japan has committed to use all policy tools—monetary, fiscal, and structural—to foster confidence and strengthen the recovery and agreed that monetary policy alone cannot lead to balanced growth. Given Japan's fragile growth outlook and weak global demand, it is increasingly important that the authorities use all policy levers, including pursuit of (1) a flexible fiscal policy in the near-term that provides a supportive fiscal impulse and (2) an ambitious structural reform agenda that prioritizes measures to lift near-term growth (such as corporate tax reform, policies to address labor market duality, and the revitalization of local economies) while continuing to move forward on reforms with longer-term benefits (such as reforms associated with the Trans-Pacific Partnership and a stronger R&D infrastructure).

Korea

Korea's current account surplus for the second half of 2015 reached $50 billion (7.4 percent of GDP), the second largest as a percent of GDP among G-20 countries, just after Germany, compared with $43 billion (6.0 percent of GDP) in the second half of 2014. For all of 2015, the current account surplus rose to 7.7 percent of GDP, from 6.0 percent of GDP in 2014. In the case of Korea,

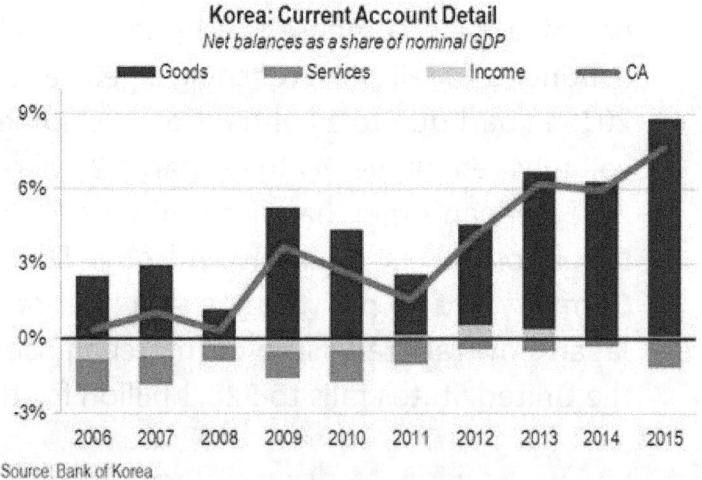

Korea: Current Account Detail
Net balances as a share of nominal GDP

Source: Bank of Korea

the larger current account surplus owed to lower import prices, particularly for energy and other commodity imports, with energy imports constituting roughly

---

[8] These include the G-7 commitments to orient fiscal and monetary policies towards domestic objectives using domestic instruments and to not target exchange rates. G-20 commitments include commitments to avoid persistent exchange rate misalignments and not target exchange rates for competitive purposes. Both the G-7 and G-20 have committed to consult closely on exchange market issues.

40 percent of Korean imports. In 2015, merchandise import volumes grew by 3.1 percent while exports rose by 2.5 percent. The growth in import volumes owes to a recovery in the housing market and fiscal stimulus introduced during the second half of the year. Korea's merchandise trade surplus with the United States totaled $13.7 billion for the last six months through December; while the combined trade and services surplus was lower, at $6.8 billion, over the same period.

Korea: Won Exchange Rates
Indexed January 2005 = 100

Source: Bank of Korea, BIS

Taiwan

Taiwan fell into recession in the middle of 2015, with a contraction of 6 percent of GDP annualized in the second quarter and a 0.2 percent contraction in the third quarter driven by a decline in exports. Economic activity picked up to 2.2 percent annualized in the fourth quarter on the announcement of an investment support program by the

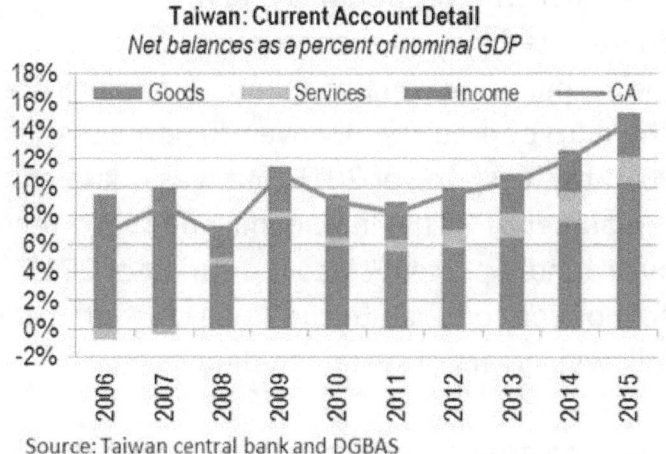

Taiwan: Current Account Detail
Net balances as a percent of nominal GDP

Source: Taiwan central bank and DGBAS

government in June and monetary easing in September. For all of 2015, GDP grew just 0.8 percent compared to 3.9 percent in 2014, with net exports subtracting 0.7 percent from overall 2015 growth as export volumes declined significantly. Despite the decline in net exports, Taiwan's goods and services trade surplus increased sharply, owing to a sharp improvement in Taiwan's terms of trade. Taiwan's current account surplus for the second half of 2015 reached $38.4 billion (15.0 percent of GDP), compared with $33.3 billion (12.4 percent of GDP) in the second half of 2014. For all of 2015, the current account surplus reached $76 billion (14.6 percent of GDP) compared to 12.4 percent of GDP in 2014. Taiwan's merchandise trade surplus with the United States totaled $6.9 billion for the last six months through December. In the balance of payments, the higher current account surplus was partially offset by financial outflows, which increased to $68 billion or 13 percent of GDP, as insurers continued to invest heavily in foreign debt instruments.

Europe

The current account surplus of the euro area expanded significantly in 2015, to 3.2 percent of GDP from 2.4 percent in 2014, driven in large part by an increase in the German current account, which increased to about 8.6 percent of GDP in 2015 from 7.4 percent in 2014. As elsewhere, much of the increase reflected lower commodity prices, but weak investment spending and a depreciated euro also contributed to the surplus. Investment spending remains 15 percent below its pre-crisis peak. The euro depreciated by over 20 percent against the dollar from the spring of 2014 to the spring of 2015, but was relatively stable against the dollar for the remainder of 2015. In nominal and real effective terms, the euro has appreciated by around 4 percent since the spring of 2015. Most euro area periphery economies continue to run small current account surpluses due to adjustments following years of sustained deficits.

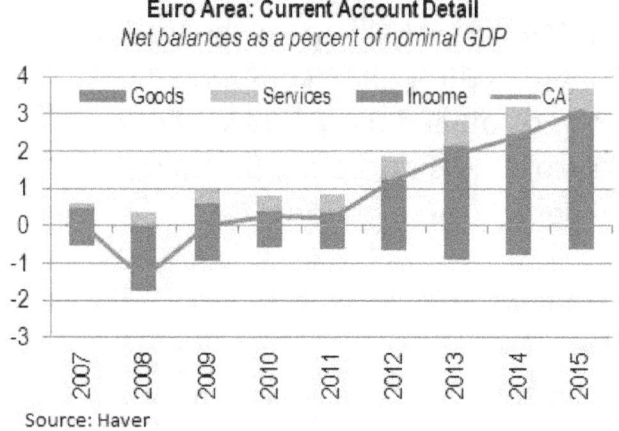

Euro Area: Current Account Detail
Net balances as a percent of nominal GDP

Source: Haver

The euro area's economy strengthened moderately in 2015, supported by low commodity prices, monetary stimulus, and a weak euro. Real GDP growth came in at 1.6 percent for the year, up from 0.9 percent in 2014. Still, the region's output remains only near its pre-crisis peak, growth decelerated in the second half of the year, and inflation remains well below the ECB's target. Therefore, it is critical for euro area economies to deploy a more balanced set of tools, including fiscal and structural policies, to provide support to domestic demand, particularly investment. Several countries—including Germany—have the fiscal space to provide more support for domestic demand. Boosting demand growth through increased fiscal support for infrastructure investment and greater private consumption is essential to sustaining the recovery of the euro area. The adjustment process, both within the euro area and globally, would function much better if countries with large current account surpluses took strong action to boost investment.

Overall global growth is being held back by (1) still high private sector leverage in some economies; (2) inadequate macroeconomic support; and (3) sluggish lending growth in some economies. Weak investment is often cited as a contributing factor to subdued global growth, but investment tends to follow GDP growth. Still, as noted, some countries could take steps to lift both private and public investment. Trade growth also has decelerated. More policy action is needed globally to strengthen demand. Monetary policy responses have been forceful in general, but they need to be supported with additional fiscal actions to deliver a stronger boost to domestic demand. Policy space exists; exceptionally low long-term interest rates provide governments with more fiscal breathing room than under historically normal circumstances. And there are a number of advanced and emerging market economies with large external surpluses (both nominal and as a share of GDP), including Germany, China, Korea, and Taiwan, that could bolster domestic demand and contribute both to stronger global growth and a more balanced global economy.

International Capital Flows

The volume of capital flows increased markedly in 2015, especially among emerging markets, and unlike most years when the flows were predominately toward emerging market economies, 2015 saw large outflows of capital from emerging markets. Outflows gained momentum especially in the second half of the year. Net outflows were particularly large from China. Most emerging economies do not provide the degree

Capital Flows to Emerging Markets

Financial Account Balance+Errors and Omissions for a group of 29 Emerging Market Economies: Source IMF + Treasury Estimates

of data disaggregation necessary to ascertain who or what is driving the flows. Private analysts estimate that roughly two thirds of recent capital outflows from China stem from repayment of foreign debt, an increase in corporate dollar deposits, and outbound Chinese FDI rather than a broader flight by Chinese residents from domestic assets or a reversal of foreign investment in China. Brazil's highly detailed balance of payments data shows that net portfolio investment by foreigners turned negative in June of 2015 and stayed negative for most of the remainder of the year. But this was due to a slowdown in gross foreign *inflows* rather than an acceleration of foreign outflows.

Advanced economies saw weaker capital flows in the latter half of 2015. In aggregate, foreign portfolio inflows to advanced economies (including from amongst themselves) turned negative beginning in the third quarter of 2015, with the sum of net foreign direct and portfolio investment in negative territory over the latter half of last year. These aggregates reflect investment between advanced

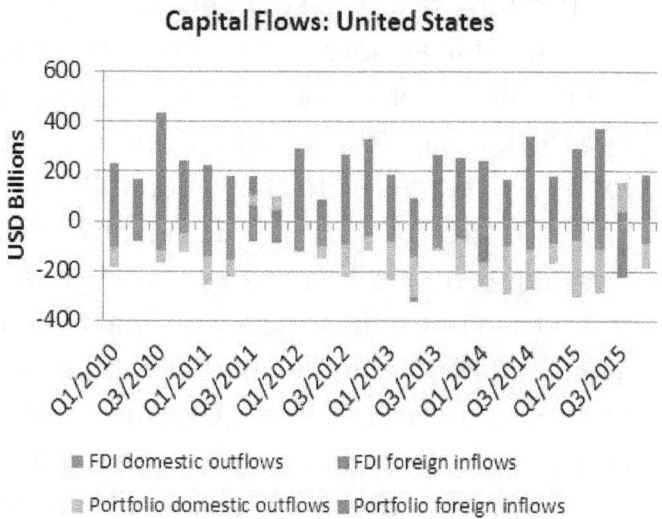

economies, and mask some economy-specific variation. Japan and the UK saw significant portfolio inflows from abroad in the second half of 2015 in the context of international market volatility, while euro area saw moderate portfolio outflows.

Global Currency Markets

Global currency markets have experienced bouts of volatility over the past six months. Through August of last year, China kept the RMB generally stable against the dollar, but as the dollar continued to strengthen against most other currencies, the RMB also appreciated on a trade-weighted basis. The unanticipated change in China's exchange rate policy in August 2015 resulted in RMB depreciation of 3 percent

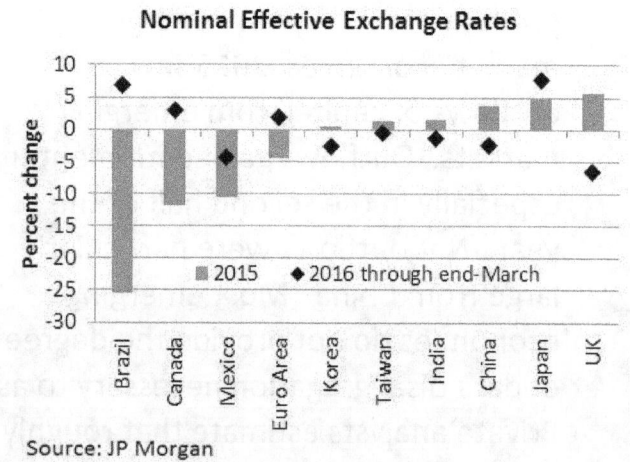

against the dollar over two days. That shift subsequently generated considerable volatility in financial markets and caused several other currencies to also depreciate against the U.S. dollar. In December, the Chinese authorities introduced a multi-currency index to re-orient markets away from the dollar-RMB bilateral exchange rate toward a trade-weighted measure of the RMB's value, but subsequently allowed the RMB to depreciate against this new index. The lack of clarity on communication about exchange rate policy, along with a weaker growth outlook, raised investor questions about the future path of the RMB. By late March 2016 the RMB had depreciated 3.8 percent against the dollar and 7 percent against the PBOC's trade-weighted China Foreign Exchange Trade System (CFETS) basket compared to early August 2015. In late February 2016, in statements to the press, China pledged to improve communications on its exchange-rate policy with the market. Chinese authorities have also stated that there is no basis for sustained devaluation of the Chinese currency.

On a nominal, trade weighted basis, emerging market currencies followed different paths over 2015. Brazil and Mexico continued on their depreciation paths which started in mid-2014. The rate of depreciation of the Mexican peso accelerated in late 2015, while the Brazilian real stabilized in the last quarter of 2015. In Asia, the path of the Indian rupee was fairly flat over the year, with a modest appreciation in the fourth quarter of 2015. In contrast, the Korean won and the new Taiwan dollar (NTD) began depreciating in mid-2015 and, like the Mexican peso, the rate of depreciation accelerated in late 2015.

Most advanced economy currencies covered in this Report began appreciating on a nominal trade-weighted basis in the latter half of 2015. Two exceptions are the Canadian dollar, where falling commodity prices in general contributed to depreciation; and the British pound, which began depreciating in late-2015 amid weaker-than-expected economic data and shifting Bank of England policy expectations, alongside uncertainty over the UK's continued membership in the European Union. In real terms, exchange rates followed similar paths over 2015.

Foreign Exchange Reserves

In the latter half of 2015, many emerging market central banks responded to capital outflows by either raising domestic interest rates or intervening in exchange markets to defend their currencies. The interventions caused central banks to dip into their stocks of foreign exchange reserves.

Measured world foreign currency reserves declined from a peak of around $12 trillion in July 2014 to about $10.9 trillion as of end-December 2015—the latest data available—a decline of $1.1 trillion. The overall decline is a combination of two developments: (1) selling of foreign currency reserves to support currencies facing depreciation pressures and (2) valuation changes in the context of changing reserve currency valuations.[9] Of the economies covered in the Report, China, Korea, and Taiwan do not publish their foreign exchange intervention activities so it is not possible to separate precisely foreign currency transactions from valuation changes.[10]

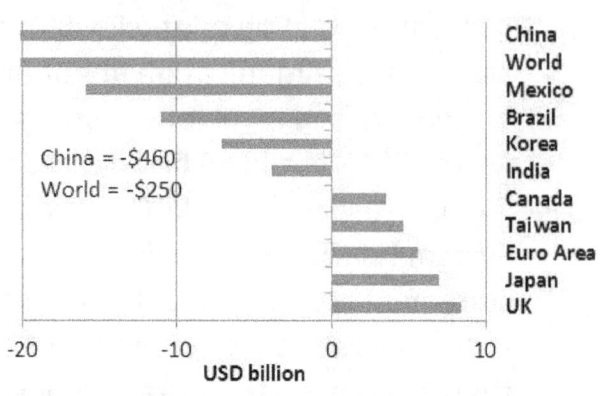

Change in Foreign Currency Reserves (end-June 2015 - end-February 2016)

China = -$460
World = -$250

China has intervened heavily in the foreign exchange markets to *support* the RMB after strong downward market pressure triggered by a surprise change in China's foreign exchange policy last August. Such a depreciation would have had negative consequences for the Chinese and global economies. More clarity over exchange rate goals and, that devaluation will not be used to support growth, would help stabilize the market. Treasury estimates that from August 2015 through March 2016, China sold more than $480 billion in foreign currency assets to support the value of the RMB.

China: FX Intervention
Billion U.S. dollar

Sources: PBOC, SAFE, U.S. Treasury estimates.

---

[9] Economies hold a basket of foreign currencies but typically report the total in U.S. dollars. When the dollar appreciates against other foreign currencies, the reported dollar value of those currencies declines.

[10] In addition, Taiwan does not currently release foreign exchange reserves information according to the IMF's Special Data Dissemination Standard (SDDS). Taiwan is not a member of the IMF but does use SDDS templates for the release of other macroeconomic and financial data.

Many other emerging market economies, including Brazil, have felt downward pressure on their currencies and have intervened as well to support their currencies. After the Mexican peso reached a record low against the dollar on February 11, 2016 on February 17, 2016 the Bank of Mexico announced a surprise hike of the policy interest rate by 0.5 percent (to 3.75 percent), indicated that it will eliminate a previous rules-based currency intervention program (started in late 2014 to support the peso), and will now undertake intervention as needed, on a discretionary basis, to respond to market volatility.

Treasury estimates that Korea intervened in the foreign exchange market in 2015 both to resist appreciation and to resist depreciation of the won during periods of financial market turbulence. For the second half of 2015 through March 2016, Treasury estimates that on net, the authorities intervened to support the won, selling an estimated $26 billion in foreign exchange, including activity in the forward and swaps market. This represented a shift from several years of

Korea: Estimate of FX Intervention

US$Bn
- FX-valuation adjusted estimate
- Change in net forward book

Source: Bank of Korea, FRB, U.S. Treasury estimates.
March forwards not yet released.

asymmetric intervention to resist appreciation. Appreciation of the won over the medium-term would help Korea reorient its economy away from its current heavy reliance on exports by encouraging the reallocation of resources to the non-tradables sector. Treasury has urged Korea to limit its foreign exchange intervention only to circumstances of disorderly market conditions. In addition, the Korean authorities should increase the transparency of their foreign exchange operations and take further steps to support domestic demand.

Treasury estimates that Taiwan's authorities continued to make net foreign currency purchases through most of 2015. Moreover, intraday foreign exchange activity suggests that the central bank continued to intervene regularly at the end of the trading day through most of 2015 to

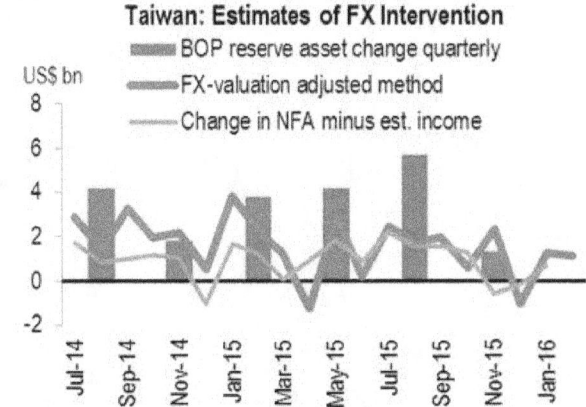

Taiwan: Estimates of FX Intervention
- BOP reserve asset change quarterly
- FX-valuation adjusted method
- Change in NFA minus est. income

US$ bn

Source: Taiwan central bank, U.S. Treasury estimates

weaken the currency. These actions suggest intervention mainly to prevent appreciation of the NTD, which would not be compatible with Taiwan's stated currency policy to smooth volatility and intervene only when the market is "disrupted by seasonal or irregular factors." Treasury estimates net foreign exchange purchases averaged $1.3 billion per month in the first ten months, followed by net foreign currency sales of $600 million in November and $140 million in December. Foreign exchange reserves totaled $426 billion (80 percent of GDP) at the end of 2015, an increase of $7 billion.

Even with sizeable foreign currency sales, as of end-2015 emerging market economies appear to be adequately reserved, with reserves more than double short term debt in all emerging market economies covered in this Report, and some over 500 percent of short term debt.

	FX reserves as % of short term debt	FX reserves as % of GDP
Brazil	597.4%	21.0%
China	536.2%	30.8%
India	382.5%	16.0%
Korea	299.9%	26.2%
Taiwan	294.2%	82.4%
Mexico	253.9%	15.4%
Japan	53.5%	28.7%
Canada	13.3%	4.5%
Euro Area	5.5%	2.1%
UK	1.8%	3.5%

Data as of end-December 2015

Section 2: Intensified Evaluation of Major Trading Partners

Key Criteria

Drawing on the discussion and analysis in the previous section, we now focus explicitly on an intensive evaluation of the criteria put forward in the provisions of the Trade Facilitation and Trade Enforcement Act of 2015 . The objective is to identify any major trading partner of the United States that has: (1) a significant bilateral trade surplus with the United States, (2) a material current account surplus, and (3) engaged in persistent one-sided intervention in the foreign exchange market.

Table 1	Bilateral goods trade balance (2015, Bil. $) (1)	Current Account		Intervention	
		Percent of GDP (2015) (2)	Memo : 3 year change percent of GDP (2a)	Net FX purchases, percent of GDP (3)	Persistent net purchases of foreign currency[1] (3a)
China	365.7	3.1%	0.5%	-3.9%*	N
Germany	74.2	8.5%	1.5%	-	N
Japan	68.6	3.3%	2.3%	0.0%	N
Mexico	58.4	-2.8%	-1.4%	-1.8%	N
Korea	28.3	7.7%	3.5%	0.2%*	N
Italy	27.8	2.2%	2.6%	-	N
India	23.2	-1.1%	3.8%	1.8%	N
France	17.6	-0.2%	1.0%	-	N
Canada	14.9	-3.3%	0.3%	0.0%	N
Taiwan	14.9	14.6%	5.0%	2.4%*	Y
UK	1.5	-5.2%	-1.9%	0.0%	N
Brazil	(4.3)	-3.3%	-0.3%	0.1%	N
Memo: Euro Area	130.2	3.2%	1.9%	0.0%	N

* Treasury Estimates

Criterion (1) - Significant bilateral trade surplus with the United States:

Column one in Table 1 provides the bilateral goods trade balances for 12 of our largest trading partners, accounting for around 70 percent of U.S. trade, for calendar year 2015.[11] China, by far, has the largest trade surplus with the United

---

[11] Although this Report does not treat the euro area itself as a major trading partner for the purposes of the Act—this Report assesses euro area countries individually—data for the euro area are presented in Table 1 and elsewhere in this Report both for comparative and contextual purposes, and because policies of the ECB, which

States, after which the size of bilateral trade surpluses declines very quickly. Treasury assesses that economies with a bilateral goods surplus of at least $20 billion (roughly 0.1 percent of U.S. GDP) have a "significant" surplus. Highlighted in red are the major trading partners that have a bilateral surplus that meets this threshold over calendar year 2015. In the aggregate, this threshold captures about 80 percent of the value of all trade surpluses with the United States.[12]

Criterion (2) - Material current account surplus:

Treasury assesses current account surpluses in excess of 3 percent of GDP to be "material" for the purposes of enhanced analysis. Highlighted in red in column 2 are the five economies that had a current account surplus in excess of 3 percent of GDP in 2015. While the change in the current account surplus over three years is not a criterion for enhanced analysis, column 2a indicates that those with the largest surpluses are also those that have seen a significant widening of their surpluses over the last three years.

Criterion (3) – Persistent, one-sided intervention:

Treasury assesses persistent, one-sided intervention to be net purchases of foreign currency, conducted repeatedly, totaling in excess of 2 percent of an economy's GDP over a period of 12 months. Columns 3 and 3a in Table 1 provide Treasury's assessment of this criterion. Numbers with an asterisk indicate Treasury estimates as these economies do not publish intervention data. Only Taiwan meets this criterion during the 12 calendar months of 2015, per Treasury estimates.

---

holds responsibility for monetary policy for the euro area, will be assessed as the monetary authority of individual euro area countries.

[12] See Section 3 for a discussion of the factors used to assess the three criteria which, taken together, would require enhanced analysis.

Summary of Findings

Pursuant to the Act,[13] Treasury finds that no economy currently satisfies all three criteria, however, five major trading partners of the United States met two of the three criteria for enhanced analysis. <u>Treasury is creating a new Monitoring List that includes these economies: China, Japan, Korea, Taiwan, and Germany</u>. China, Japan, Germany, and Korea are identified as a result of a material current account surplus combined with a significant bilateral trade surplus with the United States. Taiwan is identified as a result of its material current account surplus and its persistent, one-sided intervention in foreign exchange markets. Treasury will closely monitor and assess the economic trends and foreign exchange policies of these economies.

- China has both a significant bilateral trade surplus with the United States and a material current account surplus. China has intervened heavily in the foreign exchange markets in recent months to *support* the RMB after strong downward market pressure triggered by a surprise change in China's foreign exchange policy last August. Such a depreciation would have had negative consequences for the Chinese and global economies. More clarity over exchange rate goals, and that devaluation will not be used to support growth, would help stabilize the market. Treasury estimates that from August 2015 through March 2016, China sold more than $480 billion in foreign currency assets to support the value of the RMB. At the same time, China has a very large and growing bilateral goods trade surplus with the United States. This underscores the need for further implementation of structural reforms to rebalance the Chinese economy to household consumption, and for consumption-friendly fiscal stimulus to support demand.

- Japan has a significant bilateral trade surplus with the United States and a material current account surplus. Japan has not intervened in the foreign exchange market in over four years. Given Japan's fragile growth outlook, it is increasingly important that the authorities use all policy levers, including a flexible fiscal policy and an ambitious structural reform agenda, to lift near-term growth. Treasury assesses that current conditions in the dollar-yen foreign exchange market are orderly, and reiterates the importance of all

---

[13] Section 701 of the Trade Facilitation and Trade Enforcement Act of 2015, 19 U.S.C. § 4421.

countries adhering to their G-20 and G-7 commitments regarding exchange rate policies.

- Korea has a significant bilateral trade surplus with the United States and a material current account surplus. Treasury estimates that during the second half of 2015 through March 2016, the Korean authorities intervened to resist depreciation of the won during periods of financial market turbulence, selling an estimated $26 billion in foreign exchange, including activity in the forward and swaps market. This represented a shift from several years of asymmetric intervention to resist appreciation. Appreciation of the won over the medium-term would help Korea reorient its economy away from its current reliance on exports by encouraging the reallocation of resources to the non-tradables sector. Treasury has urged Korea to limit its foreign exchange intervention only to circumstances of disorderly market conditions. In addition, we encourage the Korean authorities to increase the transparency of their foreign exchange operations and take further steps to support domestic demand.

- Taiwan has a material current account surplus and, per Treasury estimates, has engaged in persistent net foreign currency purchases through most of 2015. In light of Taiwan's large current account surplus, such interventions are concerning. Taiwan's bilateral trade surplus with the United States, however, was not significant at less than $15 billion in 2015, and thus Taiwan did not meet all three criteria the Act establishes to advance to enhanced analysis and engagement. Nonetheless, the authorities should limit foreign exchange interventions to the exceptional circumstances of disorderly market conditions, as well as increase the transparency of reserve holdings and foreign exchange market intervention.

- Germany has both a significant bilateral trade surplus with the United States and a material current account surplus. Germany's 2015 current account surplus, valued at almost $290 billion, accounted for the bulk of the euro area's surplus, and pushed the surplus of the euro zone to over 3 percent of GDP. The European Central Bank (ECB) has not intervened in foreign currency markets since 2011, and did so then as part of a G-7 concerted intervention to stabilize the yen following Japan's earthquake and tsunami. Nonetheless, Germany has the second largest current account surplus globally,. This represents substantial excess saving—more than 8 percent of GDP—that could, at least in part, be used to support German domestic demand, while reducing the current account surplus and contributing markedly to euro-area and global rebalancing. In Treasury's view, Germany has adequate policy space to provide additional support to demand.

The fact that no major trading partner met all three criteria during this period is a reflection, in part, of the dynamics of the global economy during the past year, in which capital outflows from emerging markets have led a number of economies to engage in foreign exchange intervention to resist further *depreciation* of their currency (rather than appreciation). The extent of these flows was unusually high by historical standards, which underscores the possibility that more economies may trigger these thresholds going forward.

Treasury will continue to review the factors it uses to assess whether an economy has: (1) a significant bilateral trade surplus with the United States, (2) a material current account surplus, and (3) engaged in persistent one-sided intervention in the foreign exchange market, to ensure these new reporting and monitoring tools meet their objective of indicating where unfair currency practices may be emerging.

Section 3: New Assessment Factors for Enhanced Analysis[14]

This Section describes the factors Treasury used to assess, under Section 701(a)(2)(A)(ii) of the Trade Facilitation and Trade Enforcement Act of 2015, whether an economy that is a major trading partner of the United States has: (1) a significant bilateral trade surplus with the United States, (2) a material current account surplus, and (3) engaged in persistent one-sided intervention in the foreign exchange market.

In determining the appropriate factors to assess these criteria, Treasury took a thorough approach, analyzing data spanning 15 years across dozens of economies including all economies that have had a trade surplus with the United States during that period, and the group of economies that collectively represent 80 percent of global GDP. The discussion below presents the findings of this analysis through 2015.

Given that this is the first effort to formally implement this framework, Treasury will consult with external analysts to confirm the appropriateness of the thresholds described below. Treasury will also continue to review the factors it uses to assess these criteria to ensure that the new reporting and monitoring tools provided under the Act meet their objective of indicating where unfair currency practices may be emerging.

A. (a)(2)(A)(ii)(I) a significant bilateral trade surplus with the United States

Trade patterns are driven by a host of different factors including production costs, geographic location, geological endowments, and consumer and producer demand patterns among many other things. Accordingly, it is rare for any given economy to have balanced trade overall, or with its bilateral trading partners. In assessing what constitutes a "significant" trade surplus, Treasury analyzed the size of bilateral trade surpluses with the United States over the past 15 years.[15] The

---

[14] This Section is submitted pursuant to Section 701(a)(3) of the Trade Facilitation and Trade Enforcement Act of 2015, 19 U.S.C. § 4421.

[15] Given data limitations, we focus on trade in goods, not including services. The United States has a surplus in services trade with many countries in this Report including Canada, Brazil, China, Japan, Korea, Mexico, and the UK. Taking into account services trade would reduce the bilateral trade surplus of these countries with the United States.

economy ordering by the size of bilateral surpluses in U.S. dollars is relatively stable, and there is a rapid drop off from the largest to smaller bilateral surpluses.

The distribution of bilateral trade surpluses points to a threshold of a trade surplus of about $20 billion over the previous 12 months ending in mid- or end-calendar year to be considered "significant." This threshold would generally include the group of economies representing about 80 percent of the value of all trade surpluses with the United States, and corresponds closely to the top decile of trade surplus countries. It also captures all economies with a trade surplus with the United States that is larger than 0.1 percent of U.S. GDP. Over time, as global trade expands, this nominal figure will be reassessed to ensure it remains current and relevant.

B. (a)(2)(A)(ii)(II) a material current account surplus

An economy's current account balance reflects its trade balance and its income on assets abroad, less income it pays on foreign investment within its borders. As with trade balances, economies rarely have a balanced current account.

Treasury took an approach in assessing what is a "material" current account surplus similar to the approach it took in assessing what constitutes a "significant" bilateral trade surplus. Based on an examination of the current account balances since 2000 of all economies, and taking into account a variety of studies in the economics literature that examine the impact of current accounts as well as with the practice of other policymakers, a surplus of 3 percent of GDP is considered material. Looking at 2014 data (the last full year for which data are available on global current account surpluses), a threshold of 3 percent of GDP captures economies that account for more than half of total global current account surpluses.

This threshold is broadly consistent with a variety of studies in the economics literature that examine the impact of current accounts as well as with the practice of other policymakers.[16]

---

[16] External work that bears on this topic includes: (1) BIS working paper #169: Current Account Adjustment and Capital Flows, 2005; (2) the IMF's World Economic Outlook, October 2014, Chapter 4: Are Global Imbalances at a Turning Point?; and (3) the EU's Occasional Paper #92, Scoreboard for the surveillance of macroeconomic imbalances, 2012.

C. (a)(2)(A)(ii)(III) engaged in persistent one-sided intervention in the foreign exchange market:

Governments accumulate reserves for a range of reasons. Foreign currency reserves may be needed for day-to-day transactions including debt repayments, payments to international organizations, and payments for imports. Economies with pegged exchange rates hold reserves to counter downward pressure on their currencies. Economies with flexible exchange rates hold reserves in order to intervene in foreign exchange markets to prevent a disorderly depreciation of their currencies. Reserve holdings also can provide a defense against substantial and rapid capital outflows that could cause a loss of investor confidence and a currency crisis. At the same time, excess reserve accumulation by one or a subset of economies runs counter to the effective rebalancing of global demand, can distort the international monetary system and, by bidding up the cost of reserve assets, also makes it more expensive for vulnerable economies to build up their own precautionary buffers.

In defining what constitutes persistent, one-sided intervention, it is important to acknowledge that there are very few examples in the economic literature or policy practice to draw on as precedents. There is also no single metric by which to assess reserve levels. <u>Treasury has set a threshold for this criterion of net purchases of foreign currency, conducted repeatedly, totaling at least 2 percent of an economy's GDP over a period of 12 months ending either June or December</u>. This quantitative threshold would capture all of the major periods of foreign exchange intervention by important emerging markets since 2000. For example, based on Treasury estimates, both China and Taiwan would have met this threshold for 12 of the past 15 years, and Korea would have met the threshold for several of those years. In assessing the persistence of intervention, Treasury will consider an economy that is judged to have purchased foreign exchange on net for 8 of the 12 months to have met the threshold, although other patterns of intervention may also meet the persistence threshold.

Treasury used publicly available data for intervention on foreign asset purchases by country authorities, or as estimated by Treasury staff using valuation-adjusted foreign exchange reserves. This methodology requires assumptions about both the currency and asset composition of reserves in order to isolate returns on assets held in reserves and currency valuation moves from actual purchases and sales, including estimations of transactions in foreign exchange derivatives markets. Treasury also uses alternative data series when they provide a more accurate picture of foreign exchange balances, such as China's monthly reporting of net foreign assets on the People's Bank of China's balance sheet and Taiwan's reporting of net foreign assets at its central bank.   To the extent the assumptions made are not reflective of the true composition of reserves, estimates may over or under state intervention. Treasury strongly encourages those economies in this Report that do not currently release data on foreign exchange intervention to do so.

Glossary of Key Terms in the Report

Exchange Rate – The price at which one currency can be exchanged for another. Also referred to as the bilateral exchange rate.

Exchange Rate Regime –The manner or rules under which an economy manages the exchange rate of its currency, particularly the extent to which it intervenes in the foreign exchange market. Exchange rate regimes range from floating to pegged.

Floating (Flexible) Exchange Rate – An exchange rate regime under which the foreign exchange rate of a currency is fully determined by the market with intervention from the government or central bank being used sparingly.

Foreign Exchange Reserves – Foreign assets held by the central bank that can be used to finance the balance of payments and for intervention in the exchange market. Foreign assets consist of gold, Special Drawing Rights (SDRs), and foreign currency (most of which is held in short-term government securities). The latter are used for intervention in the foreign exchange markets.

Intervention – The purchase or sale of an economy's currency in the foreign exchange market by a government entity (typically a central bank) in order to influence its exchange rate. Purchases involve the exchange of an economy's foreign currency reserves for its own currency, reducing foreign currency reserves. Sales involve the exchange of an economy's own currency for a foreign currency, increasing its foreign currency reserves. Interventions may be sterilized or unsterilized.

Nominal Effective Exchange Rate (NEER) – A measure of the overall value of an economy's relative to a set of other currencies. The effective exchange rate is an index calculated as a weighted average of bilateral exchange rates. The weight given to each economy's currency in the index typically reflects the amount of trade with that economy.

Pegged (Fixed) Exchange Rate – An exchange rate regime under which an economy maintains a fixed rate of exchange between its currency and another currency or a basket of currencies. Typically the exchange rate is allowed to move within a narrow predetermined (although not always announced) band. Pegs are maintained through a variety of measures including capital controls and intervention.

Real Effective Exchange Rate (REER) – A weighted average of bilateral exchange rates, expressed in price-adjusted terms.

Trade Weighted Exchange Rate – see Nominal Effective Exchange Rate.